Tour of Frank Gehry Architecture & Other L.A. Buildings

D1194455

Laura Massino Smith
Architecture Tours L.A.
P.O. Box 93134 Los Angeles, CA 90093
323.464.7868
www.architecturetoursla.com

DATE DUE

Tour of Frank Gehry Architecture & Other L.A. Buildings

Laura Massino Smith

Schiffer Publishing Ltd

4880 Lower Valley Road Atglen, Pennsylvania 19310

Other Schiffer Books by Laura Massino Smith
Architecture Tours L.A. Guidebook Downtown
Architecture Tours L.A. Guidebook Hancock Park/Miracle Mile
Architecture Tours L.A. Guidebook Hollywood
Architecture Tours L.A. Guidebook Pasadena
Architecture Tours L.A. Guidebook Silver Lake
Architecture Tours L.A. Guidebook West Hollywood/Beverly Hills

Other Schiffer Books on Related Subjects
Cape May Point Three Walking Tours of Historic Cottages. Joe Jordan
Civil War Walking Tour of Savannah. David D'Arcy & Ben Mammina
South Beach Deco Step by Step. Iris Chase
Spanish Revival Architecture. "Jerry" S.F. Cook III & Tina Skinner
West Chester: Six Walking Tours. Bruce E. Mowday

Covers and book designed by: Bruce Waters
Type set in Futura Hv BT/Humanist 521 BT

ISBN: 978-0-7643-2715-5
Printed in China

Dedication

To my extraordinary husband, Drew, whose undying love, patience, encouragement, and support have guided me to discover my true passion.

Published by Schiffer Publishing Ltd.
4880 Lower Valley Road
Atglen, PA 19310
Phone: (610) 593-1777; Fax: (610) 593-2002
E-mail: Info@schifferbooks.com

For the largest selection of fine reference books on this and related subjects, please visit our web site at **www.schifferbooks.com**
We are always looking for people to write books on new and related subjects. If you have an idea for a book please contact us at the above address.

This book may be purchased from the publisher.
Include $3.95 for shipping.
Please try your bookstore first.
You may write for a free catalog.

In Europe, Schiffer books are distributed by
Bushwood Books
6 Marksbury Ave.
Kew Gardens
Surrey TW9 4JF England
Phone: 44 (0) 20 8392-8585; Fax: 44 (0) 20 8392-9876
E-mail: info@bushwoodbooks.co.uk
Website: www.bushwoodbooks.co.uk
Free postage in the U.K., Europe; air mail at cost.

Architecture Tours L.A.

Architecture Tours L.A. is a tour company that specializes in guided driving tours led by an architectural historian and driven in a 1962 vintage Cadillac. Our tours focus on the historic and significant contemporary architecture in Los Angeles and highlight the cultural aspects of the history of the built environment in Los Angeles. This guidebook will allow you to drive yourself and go about discovering L.A. in your own car and at your own pace. In addition to Frank O. Gehry, other tours offered by Architecture Tours L.A. include:

Hollywood

Silver Lake

Hancock Park/Miracle Mile

West Hollywood/Beverly Hills

Downtown Los Angeles

Pasadena

Note to Tour Goers:

The sites included on this self-guided tour are the architectural highlights in this area. This tour is meant to be an overview, a starting point of sorts, of the architecture of FRANK O. GEHRY (a.k.a. GEHRY PARTNERS) and others in the area and is intended to give the participant a feeling for the city. By no means does the tour include EVERYTHING of interest. If it did you'd be driving for days.* Instead, in a matter of hours you will be able to have a pretty good understanding of what was happening, and what is currently happening, architecturally in the Los Angeles area by the architect FRANK GEHRY. The photographs herein are for quickly identifying what you will be seeing in three dimensions. Please respect the privacy of all property owners. The criteria for inclusion are the historical, cultural, and architectural significance of a site and the fact that it can be seen easily (relatively) from the street. **So relax and have a great ride!**

*For more information, please see the bibliography.

Introduction

Frank Owen Gehry was born in Toronto, Canada, on February 28th in 1929. An early childhood influence was his grandfather's hardware store, where his grandmother would bring home scraps from the store for Gehry to play with and where he worked as a teenager. Early on in his life he developed a fascination with industrial materials. He moved to Los Angeles in 1947 with his family when he was eighteen years old. Gehry attended the University of Southern California and graduated in 1954 with a degree in architecture. After he graduated from USC and before he was drafted into the army, he changed his last name from Goldberg to Gehry at the suggestion of his first wife. Thereafter Gehry worked for Los Angeles firms, including Victor Gruen and Associates and Pereira and Luckman Associates. He also studied urban planning briefly at Harvard University's Graduate School of Design and spent a year in Paris working in the office of André Rémondet. He later returned to Santa Monica, California, and opened his own firm in 1962.

His friends, at that time, were mostly artists, including Ed Ruscha, Larry Bell, Ed Moses, and Richard Serra. He was influenced by his relationship with them and the sculptural forms of his architectural creations are evident in many of his structures. His early work from the 1960s shows an understanding of Mid-Century Modern architecture and the work of LeCorbusier and Frank Lloyd Wright. The design of his own house in 1978 marks a turning point in the transition stylistically from Modern to Post-modern. In the design of his own house, which you will soon see, he breaks up the perfect purity of the modernist box (actually a 1920s Dutch Colonial Revival House) and "explodes" the form, creating a controlled chaos. A response to and reflection of the fragmented, rapidly-moving harshness of late twentieth century life is felt in his buildings, which look and feel as though they have been broken apart. The use of inexpensive industrial materials, such as chain-link fence and corrugated steel, in residential applications earned his work the title of "Cheapskate Architecture." By using these materials as they had not been used before he created a new way of looking at architecture and pushed the boundaries of our perception of beauty in the built environment. Gehry's furniture designs in cardboard also elevate this inexpensive material to an art form. The chairs and lounges made from cardboard have proven to be very durable, very comfortable, and beautiful.

In 1989 Gehry was awarded the Pritzker Prize, the highest honor in the field of architecture, and finally started to gain international recognition as one of the world's most inventive architects. His firm has completed works of architecture in many countries in Europe and Japan, as well as the United States, and he recently purchased property in Venice, California, to build his own home from the ground up.

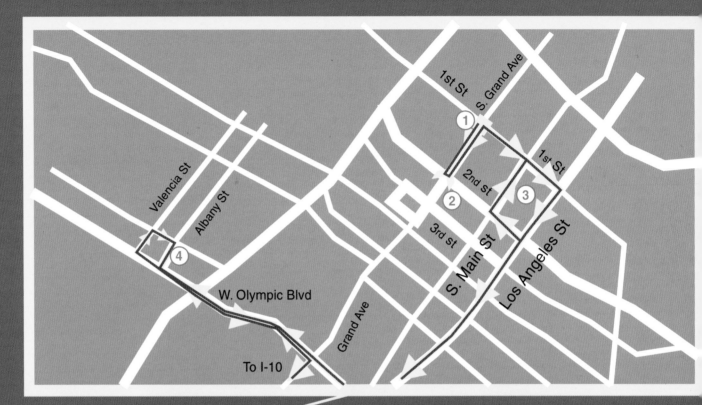

1st St

S. Grand Ave

①

1st St

2nd st

②

③

Valencia St

Albany St

3rd st

S. Main St

Los Angeles St

W. Olympic Blvd

④

Grand Ave

To I-10

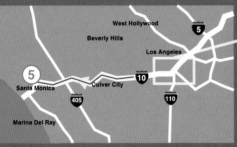

West Hollywood

Beverly Hills

Los Angeles

⑤

Santa Monica

Culver City

Marina Del Ray

Map One

151 South Grand Avenue (corner of Grand Avenue and 1st Street)

1) Completed in 2003, Walt Disney Concert Hall is the new home of the Los Angeles Philharmonic, the L.A. Master Chorale, and the Redcat Theater. Called Disney Hall because Lillian Disney, widow of Walt Disney, wanted to honor her husband's love of music and art, donating money for the creation of a concert hall. Chosen from a design competition, it was actually designed before the well-known Guggenheim Museum in Bilbao, Spain, which is of a similar shape and uses some of the same materials. The design for Disney Hall was originally revealed in 1987 and was in the planning stages for many years. Catia computer software, usually used in the automotive and aerospace industries, was used to design Disney Hall, resulting in wildly curvaceous forms. Construction was halted for a number of reasons, and then resumed after fund raising efforts in 1999. One of the reasons

1) Walt Disney Concert Hall, 2003, Gehry Partners, 151 South Grand Avenue (corner of Grand Avenue and 1st Street)

for the halt in construction came in 1994 when the 6.6 Northridge Earthquake struck, after which the building codes were altered and made more stringent.

Referred to as "frozen music," the concert hall is clad in 6,400 stainless steel panels and 3,000 polished steel panels over a 14,000-piece structural steel skeleton. A global positioning system (GPS) was used to make sure the steel supporting structure was properly in place. Conceptually, Gehry is inspired by the sails on his boat and is interested in how buildings fit into the movement of cities. Sail forms appear in the large panels, making the structure feel as though it could move. The forms resemble full-blown sails and create dramatic gestures. The panels also mimic the lines on sheet music making a connection to musical performance. Gehry sees architecture as artistic composition and nowhere is this more apparent than here. He breaks up the box by using sweeping, curving forms and almost no ninety-degree angles. On the side of the structure that faces Hope Street, the Founders' Room is expressed on the exterior in very shiny, chrome-like

polished stainless steel panels, which, at one point, were reflecting the sun so intensely that the apartments across the street were heating up. The panels had to be burnished so they would not be as reflective. Nicknamed "Los Angeles' Living Room," Disney Hall is accessible to those walking by the human-scale glass wall as they are able to see what is inside. A rooftop garden is located in back and is open for everyone to enjoy. Lillian Disney loved flowers and the garden was created for her and the residents of the city as a peaceful, green refuge amongst the harsh urban environment of Downtown L.A. Directly adjacent to the concert hall is a limestone clad rectilinear structure that houses the Los Angeles Philharmonic Association. Designed by architects Chu + Gooding, the form and color of the building are in complete contrast with the concert hall, but co-exist unobtrusively. With the completion of Walt Disney Concert Hall, the skyline of Los Angeles has been changed forever and a new dynamic abstract sculptural dimension has been added.

1) Walt Disney Concert Hall, 2003, Gehry Partners, 151 South Grand Avenue (corner of Grand Avenue and 1st Street) above & right

Across the street from the concert hall to the west:

2) The Museum of Contemporary Art was designed by Japanese architect Arata Isozaki and completed in 1986. MOCA was the first building in the United States designed by Isozaki. The form of the structure in pure geometric shapes with squares, semi-circles, and pyramids creates a visually stimulating composition. Covered in red Indian clay stone, the administrative offices are located above ground, while all of the galleries are below creating as much wall space as possible for exhibition and using pyramid-shaped sky-lights that allow natural light into the galleries. MOCA is the primary museum for contemporary art in Los Angeles. Frank Gehry transformed an old warehouse in Little Tokyo into what was then called the Temporary Contemporary branch of MOCA in 1983, now known as the Geffen Contemporary Museum and functioning as an additional branch of MOCA.

(See additional sites, p. 63)

2) Museum of Contemporary Art (MOCA), 1986, Arata Isozaki with Gruen Associates, 250 South Grand Avenue

From Grand Avenue, head east, turn right on 1st Street, pass Main Street, right on Los Angeles Street:

3) Filling the entire block bordering 1st Street, Los Angeles Street, 2nd Street, and Main Street is a recent structure designed by Thom Mayne-Morphosis, the recipient of the Pritzker Prize, the highest honor in architecture. Cal Trans, as it is also known, is the government organization responsible for the region's roads and highways. This building is thirteen stories high and encloses 716,200 square feet in addition to underground parking. It houses 1,850 Caltrans employees and 500 City of Los Angeles Department of Transportation employees. Unique building elements are seen here, including a "skip-stop" elevator, which only stops on every third floor as well as an outdoor lobby. The skip-stop elevator was conceived as a way for employees to interact more with each other as they use the stairs to get to their destination. The outdoor lobby has a four-story light sculpture created by artist Keith Sonnier called "Motordom." Red and blue neon light strips are arranged in a horizontal pattern mimicking that of the crowded freeways with taillights of cars as seen at night from a time-lapsed photograph. Along the outside of the building there is a metal scrim comprised of perforated aluminum panels. The panels are controlled by a computer and timed to open and close at optimum moments to allow sunlight in or to shut it out. Energy is generated from the photovoltaic cells on the south side of the building facing 2nd Street, which produce about five percent of the energy the building needs. A super graphic number 100 marks the entrance on Main Street and the street address of the building. This building has been awarded a Silver LEED (Leadership in Energy and Environmental Design) rating because of its design consideration regarding energy usage.

3) California Department of Transportation District 7 Headquarters Building (Cal Trans), 2004, Thom Mayne-Morphosis, 100 South Main Street

Right on 2nd Street, right on Main Street, right on 1st Street and right again on Los Angeles Street, right on Olympic Blvd., pass Figueroa Street to Albany Street:

4) Between Albany Street and Valencia Street on Olympic Blvd. is an ongoing project started in the mid'70s. Difficult to see here, and even more difficult to penetrate, is the Loyola University Law School. Gehry developed a master plan that began in 1978. It has been an ongoing and expanding project since then. Gehry uses contemporary interpretations of Classical forms, including columns, pediments, and towers. In this case, the columns have no decoration and don't conform to a specific Classical order of architecture such as Doric or Ionic. They are simply made of concrete and/or galvanized metal, left bare, and are truncated. The use of various bright colors including yellow, orange, and green add to the liveliness of the campus. This kind of architecture is considered to be the Historic Eclectic side of Post-modern architecture. Conceptually using the ancient idea of the village, like a civic center, where traditional forms such as temples and pyramids create the basis of the design, but offers a reinterpretation of these forms. In this way, historical precedents are acknowledged and brought forward into contemporary life.

4) Loyola University Law School, 1978-present, Gehry Partners, 1441 West Olympic Blvd.

26th St

Washington Ave

Santa Monica Blvd

⑥

26th St

22nd St

Santa Monica Blvd

Washington Ave

⑤

Cloverfield Blvd

🛡10

Colorado Ave

Lincoln Blvd

6th St

🛡10

⑦

4th St

2nd St

Broadway

Map Two

⑧

Right on Valencia Street, right on James M. Wood Blvd., right on Albany Street, left on Olympic Blvd., right on Grand Avenue, right on 17th Street to 10 Freeway West (Santa Monica Freeway) entrance, merge onto freeway, exit at Cloverfield Blvd. North, right on Cloverfield Blvd., just past Colorado Ave., before Broadway, look to your left:

5) On your left are the former offices of Frank Gehry. Ten thousand feet of an existing warehouse were remodeled for use as the architect's offices, complete with model shop and printing facilities as well as the usual design studio. The signature galvanized sheet metal panels are seen on the outside. This space was occupied by Gehry's firm up until 2002, when the firm moved east to larger quarters near Culver City.

5) Former Gehry Offices, 1987 until 2002, Gehry Partners, 1520 Cloverfield Blvd.

Having exited the freeway, you are now in the City of Santa Monica. Located about sixteen miles from Downtown Los Angeles, Santa Monica was incorporated in 1886 and named for Saint Monica. The Tongva Indians were native to this area, after which there were enormous Mexican farms called Rancho San Vicente y Santa Monica and another called Rancho Boca de Santa Monica. The 1880s, however, saw the proliferation of development in the form of hotels and homes and in 1890 the population was a little more than 1,500. By 1900 the population grew to over 3,000. In 1897 the United States Congress chose San Pedro Bay, about thirty miles south, as the Port of Los Angeles instead of Santa Monica Bay as the major port of commerce for southern California. Santa Monica thrived as a seaside resort since its scenic beauty was unspoiled by a busy port. Amusement piers were built and residents of Downtown Los Angeles would take the streetcar out to the coastal beach towns of Santa Monica and Venice for the weekends. During the strong economy of the 1920s, many upscale resort hotels were built that still exist today. In 1921, the Douglas Aircraft Company was founded here on the location of what is now the Santa Monica Airport. The DC-3 commercial plane was developed there. During World War II, the Douglas Aircraft Company built many planes and employed many people. Growth continued after World War II and in 1950 the population was over 71,000. The Santa Monica Freeway was completed in 1966 and created a fast connection to all points from Santa Monica. The poor economy of the 1960s and '70s saw a downturn in neighborhoods and commercial districts; however, a number of historic houses threatened with demolition were salvaged. At the same time a fitness craze was prominent in Santa Monica. A bicycle path adjacent to the beach was constructed and actress Jane Fonda opened an aerobics studio. With the 1980s, restoration began on some of the older buildings and new shopping centers were built and thrived into the 1990s. Large companies like MTV, Universal, Google, and Yahoo are all located in Santa Monica. In 1994 Bergamot Station, an old train station, was converted to art galleries and is a center of art for the city today. The population in Santa Monica since 2000 was more than 85,000 and is expected to rise. The City of Santa Monica even has its own logo, which can be seen on the street sign poles. Depicted inside a circular disk are the sun, the mountains, and the ocean. Many structures designed by Frank Gehry are located in Santa Monica, as is his own house, coming up next.

Right on Santa Monica Blvd., left on 26th Street, left on Washington Avenue to 22nd Street:

6) At the southwest corner of Washington Avenue and 22nd Street is Gehry's own home. It began life as a 1920s Dutch Colonial Revival style house, complete with gambrel roof, characteristic of that popular style of the 1920s, and was expanded around 1978. In this first renovation, the house was wrapped with industrial-type materials, including corrugated metal, chain link fencing, safety glass, and exposed wood. Glass window/walls have been constructed to look precarious through the use of odd angles and crashing intersections. Conceptually and literally the structure has been taken apart and the raw wood framing has been left exposed. Within the house, some of the plaster was removed to reveal the wood framework, revealing the "bones" of the structure. This is visible in the upper pitch of the roof on the side of the house where a glass window/wall has replaced the wall and shingling exposing the wood structure behind. The intentionally unsettling form of this house expresses the anxiety of living in a crowded, chaotic, fragmented late twentieth century world. With this work of architecture, Gehry shocked us through the use of materials once considered to be used only in heavy industry. He showed that they can have a sculptural beauty and can even be used in a residential setting. Also shocking is the overall shape of the house. It is a reinterpretation of what a house can look like and of what it can be made. Gehry was also interested in deconstructing the traditional form of the house the pure geometry of the Modernist box of the '50s and '60s and questioning accepted modes of construction and materials, shown here by keeping the older structure in place and introducing new forms. Intrigued with the idea of "the process of construction," he believed that a building was more interesting during the construction process before it was finished and covered over with walls, hiding the inner workings. This type of architecture is considered to be the Deconstructivist side of Post-modern architecture. Some have compared this to the Cubism Movement found in painting and sculpture where images are fragmented and then shuffled back together.

A later renovation in the early 1990s involved the addition of landscaping, a pool, and a guest house.

6) Gehry House, 1978, Gehry Partners, 1002 22nd Street

6) Gehry House, 1978, Gehry Partners, 1002 22nd Street

Continue on Washington Avenue, left on Lincoln Blvd., right on Broadway to 6th Street:

7) At the northeast corner of Broadway and 6th Street, on your right, is a residential complex with a restaurant and retail shop on the first floor. Completed in 2002, these apartments use steel decking material as an exterior decorative element. The idea of using industrial materials decoratively is an idea of Gehry's seen in the creation of his house in the late 1970s and being carried out here more than twenty years later. Gehry's influence has been very far-reaching worldwide, but especially visible in southern California.

7) Breeze Suites Moderne, 2002, John G. Reed, Don E. Empakeris/REA Architects, 609 Broadway

Continue on Broadway to 4th Street:

8) Beginning at the southwest corner of 4th Street on Broadway is the Santa Monica Place shopping mall. This retail center was completed not long after his own house. (The two major anchor stores were designed by the retailer's own architects, however.) The angled greenhouse-like glass structure, which is the entrance to the mall, also marks the starting point of the pedestrian Third Street Promenade shopping center. The massing of the buildings is organized in such a way that it breaks up the urban street grid, by placing the buildings on an angle. Parts of the walls have been cut out to give views of the building inside, making it inviting to people walking by. Within the complex, Gehry again breaks up the box using a system of angles that create interest while negotiating the stores. The use of skylights also lets the outside in. On the southwest end, a fine chain link fence is used to envelope the parking structure and layered over that in huge block letters of chain link are the words "Santa Monica Place," seen on Colorado Ave. There has been discussion in 2007 of a renovation of this shopping center.

8) Santa Monica Place, c. 1980, Gehry Partners, 315 Broadway

8) Santa Monica Place, c. 1980, Gehry Partners, 315 Broadway (above & left)

Map Three

Colorado Ave

Main St

Pico Blvd

Main St

Ocean Park Blvd

Marine St

Main St

Sunset Ave

Indiana Ave

Hampton Dr

4th Ave

Electric Ave

Abbot Kinney Blvd

Venice Blvd

⑨ ⑩ ⑪ ⑫ ⑬ ⑭ ⑮ ⑯ ⑰ ⑱ ⑲ ⑳ ㉑ ㉒ ㉓

Left on 2nd Street, left on Colorado Ave., quick right on Main Street:

9) On your left is Santa Monica City Hall. Donald Parkinson was one of the architects of the Bullocks-Wilshire Department Store on Wilshire Blvd. and Union Station in Downtown L.A. This location was originally intended to be a central focal point for a grouping of civic buildings that were never built. The Late Art Deco style called Streamline Moderne is seen in this building. The Great Depression of the 1930s created a pared down version of the more elaborate Art Deco style of the 1920s. During the economic boom, however, before the stock market crash of 1929, many Americans were traveling more by car, train, and ocean liner and that obsession with speed and movement is reflected in the design of this building.

9) Santa Monica City Hall, 1939, Donald Parkinson and J.M. Estep, 1685 Main Street

Continue on Main Street:

10) RAND Headquarters, 2005, DMJM Design, 1776 Main Street

10) Next on your right is the recently completed RAND Headquarters office building. The convex curve of the building follows the contours of the street. This reflects the two arcs of the building; one is visible from the street. A courtyard is created in the center of the two arcs and natural light and air are accessible to each office through the use of operable windows. A continuous circular pattern of circulation throughout the structure is achieved here through the use of bridges and connections at the ends of the arcs. The circular form also corresponds to the non-hierarchal organization of RAND and creates a democratic arrangement. Materials used on the exterior include precast concrete, cement, plaster, metal, and glass, creating a repeating geometric pattern.

Continue on Main Street:

11) Next on your left, recognized since 2002 as a Santa Monica City Landmark, the Mid-Century Modern auditorium is shielded in a perforated concrete wall with seventy-two-foot high concrete masts—looking like they could hold sails and take off into the nearby ocean. The height of them adds to the drama of the building, making it stand out as an important civic structure. Well-known local architect Welton Becket also designed the Capitol Records Building in Hollywood, the Beverly Hilton Hotel in Beverly Hills, and was one of the architects on the "Theme Building" at L.A. International Airport.

11) Santa Monica Civic Auditorium, 1959, Welton Becket and Associates, Main Street and Pico Blvd.

Continue on Main Street:

12) Here on your right, at the southwest corner of Main Street and Pico Blvd., is a small-scale office building designed by local architects from an existing warehouse. The use of the clear glass on the upper portion serves as a unifying border and also shows the observer the framing structure referencing Gehry's idea of exposing the structure through glass. Below we see the use of perforated horizontal galvanized metal panels as a decorative and practical solution for sheathing the lower portion of the building. Used this way, creating privacy inside, away from the busy street outside, but light is still able to filter through to the inside.

12) Pico Main Building, 1997, DalyGenik (Kevin Daly & Chris Genik), 1901 Pico Blvd.

Continue on Main Street, just past Hollister Avenue, turn left into the Edgemar Development and park there:

13) Here on your left is another complex designed by Gehry, circa 1988. In Gehry's original design, the first home of the Santa Monica Museum of Art, now located at Bergamot Station, was here. The liberal use of angles, especially at the street entrance, is evident here. One is meant to enter through the sidewalk on a curved angle. The massing of the structure and the use of chain link fence, galvanized sheet metal, and diamond plate flooring—another industrial material—are typical choices. He has also created towers here to suggest a central focal point, but they also function as roadside architecture, which attracts your eye as you drive by. The central plaza serves as a gathering place, which is shielded from the street, but open in the center. Originally on this site was the Edgemar Farms Dairy and an original part of the dairy,

now rebuilt, exists on the right side facing the street in the green tiled building. Another material seen here is what we would consider to be interior bathroom tile. Again, the use of a material usually considered for interior residential use is here in an exterior public/commercial installation defying conventional modes of thinking.

13) Edgemar Development, c. 1988, Gehry Partners, 2415 Main Street

Continue south on Main Street:

14) On your left, just in from the corner of Ocean Park Blvd. and Main Street, is a beautiful Late Art Deco style Streamline Moderne office building. Resembling an ocean liner, appropriate for its proximity to the ocean, it has a nautical theme that was used in other buildings of this period, including The Coca-Cola Bottling Plant in Downtown L.A., completed the same year, and the Santa Monica City Hall a few years later. The offices of Merle Norman Cosmetics were originally housed here.

14) Merle Norman Building, 1936, George Parr, 2525 Main Street

Continue on Main Street:

15) Next on your left at the northeast corner of Marine Street and Main Street is an office building composed of brown brick and steel. James Tyler was one of the principal architects working with Craig Ellwood. Ellwood is known as the architect of Art Center College of Design in Pasadena, which Tyler also claims credit for. Elwood's work throughout Los Angeles embodies the Mid-Century Modern aesthetic with pure geometric massing, usually perfect rectangular-shaped cubes, and the liberal use of glass curtain walls. His signature element was the use of brick instead of masonry walls between the glass. As you can see, brown brick is used here, along with glass and steel. This structure also seems to float above the ground as it is elevated on structural columns. The building is reminiscent of the aesthetic of International Style architect Mies van der Rohe, who designed the Barcelona Pavilion and the Farnsworth House, which have become Mid-Century Modern icons.

15) Main/Marine Center, 1987, James Tyler, 3015 Main Street

Continue on Main Street:

You've just crossed the border of the City of Santa Monica and are now in the neighborhood that is part of the City of Los Angeles known as Venice.

From the years 1904 through 1906, "Venice-of-America" was created as an entertainment and amusement resort, inspired by Venice, Italy, and thought of as the Coney Island of the West. It was the dream of wealthy tobacco grower Abbot Kinney to re-invent Venice, Italy, here and in doing so he had an elaborate system of canals and lagoons built, as well as an amusement pier. The canals were filled with water and gondolas, complete with imported Italian gondoliers. Arcades were replicated here from the Piazza San Marco in Venice, Italy, and remnants of them can still be found. Architects Norman Marsh and C. H. Russell created much of the design. The Pacific Electric Venice Short Line brought visitors here from Downtown L.A., where most of the people of the city were living. People flocked to this seaside resort. At the time, Kinney's ultimate plan was to get people here to have fun and hopefully sell the surrounding plots of land to them. Venice-of-America was very successful for a long time, but Kinney's death in 1920, followed by a succession of fires and Prohibition, took their toll.

In 1925 Venice, which was originally a separate city, was annexed to the city of Los Angeles and the amusement piers were affected by the city's blue laws, which contained anti-gambling statutes and banned Sunday dancing. Although other amusement piers exist to the present, most of the canals were filled in, paved over, and made into roads by 1930. Those canals south of Venice Blvd., including Carroll, Linnie, Eastern, Howland, and Sherman, were not filled in due to the onset of the Great Depression. Oil was discovered, however, during this time and at one time the southern part of Venice was filled with oilrigs. In 1946, the Venice amusement pier was dismantled because of opposition from the City of Los Angeles.

In the '60s artists started moving in for the cheap rents and the area has remained a center of art and beach culture. Venice, however, has always been a place of very high creativity and many artists have their studios here, including Ed Ruscha, Laddie John Dill, and Robert Graham. One of the oldest art galleries in the city, called L.A. Louver, is also here and many architecture and creative media firms are currently located in Venice. Gehry's new home will be built in this area.

16) On your right at the northwest corner of Rose Avenue and Main Street is a mixed use development. This condominium and retail complex, built in the late 1980s, was based on the original Venice-of-America design. Parts of the arcade were reproduced and you can see here the columns with the capitals displaying the face of a man thought to be the creator of Venice himself, Abbot Kinney. The molds, however, strangely were supposedly created from the face of a seventeen-year-old girl by Italian sculptor Felix Peano. Here they were replicated from the original molds paying homage to the early days of Venice. The "Ballerina Clown" sculpture facing the intersection is now a well-known visual landmark meant to portray a sense of the character of the current Venice, combining fine arts and amusement arts. The sculpture form is also a reference to the history of Venice as an amusement center.

16) Venice Renaissance Building, 1989, Van Tilburg, Branvard & Soderbergh, ("Ballerina Clown" sculpture, Jonathan Borofsky), 255 Main Street

16) Venice Renaissance Building, 1989, Van Tilburg, Branvard & Soderbergh, 255 Main Street

Continue on Main Street:

17) On your left, past Rose Avenue, is one of Gehry's most publicized buildings, often referred to as "The Binoculars Building." It is another visual landmark on Main Street. This structure was built originally to house the offices of the Chiat/Day advertising agency. They were founded in Los Angeles in 1968 and eventually expanded in 1980 with offices in New York. In 1988 they merged with the Australian advertising company called "Mojo." No longer here, however, the building now houses offices for other advertising firms. The form of the building is fragmented. Facing straight on, the left side is encased in white metal and suggestive of the bow-form of a ship, which relates to the proximity of the ocean blocks away. The central brick form behind the binoculars recedes and becomes a setting for the huge binoculars sculpture and the copper vertical forms on the right were intended to resemble trees. Function is what ties them all together. The oversized sculpture in front was created by Claes Oldenburg and Coosje van Bruggen and serves as the entrance marker, where cars can enter the parking structure and people walk in. These artists are well known for their giant versions of just about everything from a hot water bottle to a Swiss Army knife complete with movable parts. Within the enormous binoculars is usable space with a circular skylight on top and an attached walkway to the main building.

Oddly enough, the idea of the binoculars was actually from another collaboration with the artists and Gehry, but when looked at again seemed to fit perfectly in this space. Advertising is a metaphorical magnification of products so an analogy can be drawn. This is another example of "roadside" architecture, however, because the sculpture boldly catches your eye as you drive by. The sheer size of the binoculars and the vertical copper elements jutting out above the street create a jarring visual dynamic. The incongruous shapes and materials chosen create an exciting presence, as well as the choice of colors—white, black, and copper. The fragmented parts of the building create a juxtaposition of forms, which make a strong visual and sculptural statement.

17) Chiat/Day Building, (now Ketchum Advertising; Tribal DBB), 1991, Gehry Partners ("Binoculars" sculpture—Claes Oldenburg & Coosje Van Bruggen), 340 Main Street

Left on Sunset Avenue:

18) These loft residences at the southeast corner of Main Street and Sunset Avenue are live/work spaces, zoned for both residential and commercial purposes. Designed by a local architect who has also designed the Goodwill Building in Hollywood—there with exposed I-beams, insulation, ductwork, and large expanses of glass in the Deconstructivist manner. Here, envisioned as an artist's colony, the interior spaces are enormous and flooded with light. They are able to accommodate the creation of large-scale paintings and sculpture and with a utility core (kitchen/bath) can be configured almost any way. Located in a neighborhood with many existing artist's studios, this complex was meant to blend with the neighborhood as if it had always been there even though it was recently completed. Exterior courtyard spaces were designed for performances with an area that could function as a stage. The circula-tion of the complex was designed with the intention of creating an interactive community so neighbors could see each other and converse. Comprised of forty-nine units and two commercial spaces, the exteriors are surfaced in vertical metal ribbed siding and large expanses of glass.

18) Venice Art Lofts, 2004, aARts William Dale Brantley Architects Inc., 615 Hampton Drive

Right on Hampton Drive, left on Indiana Avenue:

19) Here at the southeast corner of Hampton Avenue and Indiana Avenue are the Hampton Court condominiums designed by another local architect who once worked in the office of Frank Gehry. Also intended for use by artists to accommodate large-scale artwork, the ceiling heights go to 14'-6". The roofs are angled to increase the height of the ceilings and to create large glass windows that allow natural light in. The extended rooflines, exposed rafters, pure geometric forms, and glass all refer to the design concepts of Mid-Century Modernism. The intense coloration reinforces the individuality of each building while providing visual interest to the street. The Hampton Court project was awarded the 2003 Community Enrichment Award by the Southern California Development Forum.

19) Hampton Court, 2002, Frederick Fisher and Partners, 800-804 Hampton Avenue and 320 Indiana Avenue

Directly adjacent to Hampton Court further on your right:

20) These structures were designed for three artists on a narrow lot and set up almost like townhouses with one house tightly adjacent to the other. They are comprised of three separate 1500 square foot studios, which are also living spaces. The various shapes and materials, including stucco, exposed plywood, and asphalt shingles make each unit distinct. The use of exaggerated forms is also a favorite device of Gehry's. Notice the stepped corner that looks like a toppling staircase. On the interior, it is expressed in its raw form with exposed wood.

20) Indiana Avenue Studios, 1981, Gehry Partners, 326 Indiana Avenue

Directly adjacent to Indiana Avenue Studios:

21) Next door is the Hopper House belonging to the actor, artist, and photographer Dennis Hopper. The corrugated metal facade with no windows makes it uninviting to the street, which also makes the focus of the house on the interior. Like a fortress, the use of industrial materials adds to the hard urban feeling of this area. The white picket fence is the only element that alludes to the traditional idea of a house and provides a contrast in materials juxtaposed against the metal.

21) Hopper House, 1989, Brian Murphy (BAM), 330 Indiana Avenue

Right on 4th Avenue, left on Electric Avenue, quick right on Westminster Avenue, left on Abbot Kinney Blvd.:

22) On your right, at the corner of Andalusia Avenue and Abbot Kinney Blvd., are three condominium units designed for the use of artists as homes and studios. Zoned as live/work lofts, inside each unit is 4,000 square feet of adaptable open space. The front facade is a flat planar surface with concrete blocks, stainless steel, glass, and very colorful stucco resembling the rectilinear composition of a Mondrian painting and making the three-unit complex appear as one.

22) Abbot Kinney Lofts, 2001, Mark Mack, Tim Sakamoto, Jeff Allsbrook, 1318-1320-1324 Abbot Kinney Blvd.

Continue on Abbot Kinney Blvd.:

23) Next on your right, just past California Avenue at the corner of Navarra Court, is a small office building. Originally commissioned by a South African developer, tenants were Machine Head, a sound and music design office, and Ravenswork, a creative advertising firm. The yellow painted stucco surface is combined with stone panels and, up above, notice the accordion-shaped, glass light towers, which allow natural light into the space and create a dynamic sculptural form in glass. The facade is divided into three distinct layers. The yellow stucco portion at ground level with rectangular windows is below a second portion of stone panels and the third part is of geometric sculptural form with unique glass windows providing ample light and an opening overhead to the sky.

23) 1410 Abbot Kinney Building, 2002, Mulder/Katkov (Miriam Mulder-project architect), 1410 Abbot Kinney Blvd.

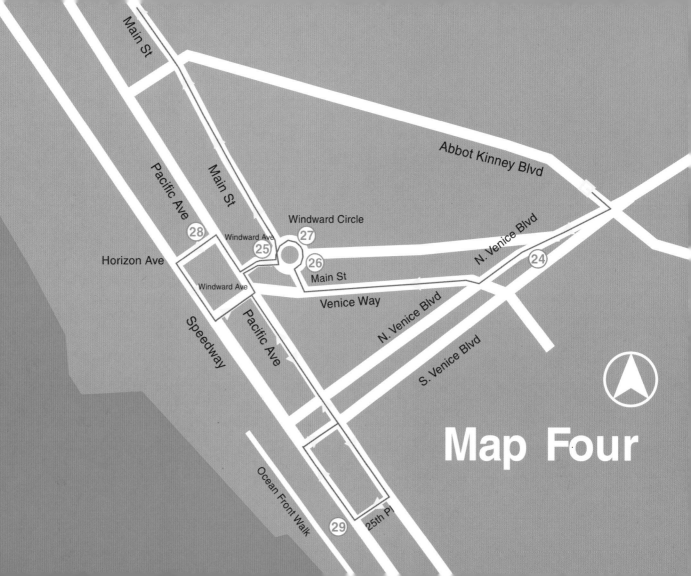

Main St

Abbot Kinney Blvd

Pacific Ave

Main St

Windward Circle

28

25 Windward Ave 27

Horizon Ave

N. Venice Blvd

26

24

Windward Ave

Main St

Speedway

Venice Way

Pacific Ave

N. Venice Blvd

S. Venice Blvd

Ocean Front Walk

29 25th Pl

Map Four

43

Continue on Abbot Kinney Blvd., right on Venice Blvd.:

24) Coming up quickly on your left is the public library named for the founder of Venice. This was constructed on property owned by the city to replace an older library building that was outgrown by the community. This project was originally designed by East Coast architect, Michael Graves, who also designed some of the Walt Disney Studio buildings in Burbank. However, at the completion of the project, Graves did not want his name associated with the building because of changes that were made out of accordance with his original design. Ernest P. Howard & Associates, a southern California architect, also worked on the project. The interesting qualities of the structure are the natural timber supports encasing glass, which allow the light to filter through. This superstructure enveloping the building creates a sense of stability and strength with the tower-like element on the top and alludes to the structure of the original amusement piers of early Venice as though you were

looking at the underside of the pier. Inside, the forty-foot high central hall terminates in the octagonal shaped tower on the end, which addresses the corner by conforming to its site. The various building shapes are unified by the pinkish stucco and blue tiles.

24) Abbot Kinney Memorial Branch of the Los Angeles Public Library, 1995, Michael Graves; Ernest P. Howard & Associates (principal architect William Holland), 501 South Venice Blvd.

Right on Venice Way, right on Main Street, around Windward Circle halfway to the other side of Main Street:

Stop and park to look at the next three buildings.

25) Windward Circle was where the "Venice Lagoon" once was, which was filled in 1929. Abbot Kinney's home was here on the edge of the circle. Grand Boulevard was once "The Grand Canal," a reference to the large canal in Venice, Italy of the same name. Three buildings designed by a local architect are all, in some way, referential to the history of Venice. The Ace Market's (now 1501 Main) large disc and pulley decorative elements are meant to allude to the giant steam shovels with which the canals of Venice were dug. Replicas of the original columns with decorative capitals from the original Venice-of-America exist here, too.

25) Windward Circle: Ace Market (now 1501 Main), c. 1989, Steven Ehrlich Architects, 185 Windward Avenue, 1501 Main Street

26) The circular building is intended to give the feeling of the roller coaster that was once part of the original amusement park. This can be seen in the arched slide form between the circular section and the squared section of the building.

27) Finally, the Arts Building, with its concave façade, is located where there once was a hotel. Over the years it has functioned as artists' studios, then a single-family home, and an art gallery. The culvert pipes used here, look both like huge screws, in a post-industrial aesthetic, and mimic Classical architectural columns.

27) Windward Circle: Windward Circle Arts Building, 1988, Steven Ehrlich Architects, 211 Windward Avenue

26) Windward Circle: Race Through the Clouds, c. 1989, Steven Ehrlich Architects, 1600 Main Street

Continue straight onto Windward Avenue, towards the ocean, right on Pacific Avenue, left on Horizon Avenue:

28) Spiller House, 1980, Gehry Partners, 39 Horizon Avenue

28) Here on your right on this narrow lot, is the Spiller House, commissioned by Jane Spiller as a private family residence and a rental unit. Again, inexpensive industrial materials are used in such a way as to raise them to a level of beauty, not seen before. The house is almost completely clad in unpainted corrugated metal, with exposed wood studs peeking through the windows. Colliding planes intersecting at the very top serve to break up the series of boxes that comprise this house. A central courtyard separates the two parts of the house and the roof is used as an outdoor living space affording views of the ocean.

Continue on Horizon Avenue, left on Speedway, left on Windward Avenue, right on Pacific Avenue, right on 25th Place (25th Place dead ends in the next site; you may want to park and walk along Ocean Front Walk to see the front of this house):

29) On the ocean side of this house is the busy Venice Boardwalk. With many people walking by every day, the challenge of design was to create privacy, but also retain the views. This was achieved through the use of a short cinderblock wall and blocks of structures. The back portion is also set back from the boardwalk to allow for privacy and a rooftop terrace. Near the front and elevated on a single column is a reinterpretation of a lifeguard tower, here with retractable

shades for privacy. The mixture of materials used creates a visually entertaining composition. A log gate in front marking the entrance, ceramic tiles like those in a kitchen or bathroom interior, and stucco and concrete block are all incongruous elements reflecting the eclectic nature of everything around.

29) Norton House, c. 1984, Gehry Partners, 2509 Ocean Front Walk

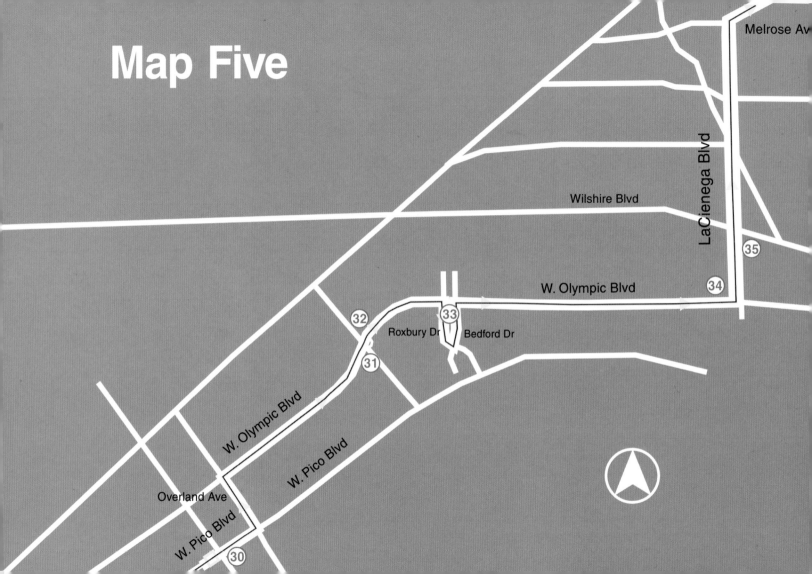

Map Five

Melrose Av

LaCienega Blvd

Wilshire Blvd

35

34

W. Olympic Blvd

32

33

Roxbury Dr   Bedford Dr

31

W. Olympic Blvd

W. Pico Blvd

Overland Ave

W. Pico Blvd

30

Right on Speedway, right on South Venice Blvd., left on Pacific Avenue, right on Windward Avenue, around the circle, right on Main Street, right on Pico Blvd. pass the 10 Freeway, pass the 405 Freeway, past Westwood Blvd.:

30) Now we move out of Venice and Santa Monica and into the area known as West L.A. On the right side of the street is a large shopping mall designed in the mid-'80s by the same firm that designed Universal City Walk near Hollywood and other urban retail centers. Originally a one-level suburban style retail center, it was expanded by almost 300,000 square feet. In order to create an urban marketplace, a three-story pedestrian oriented complex was created. On the interior, a 550-foot high central skylight creates a canopy of sorts, flooding the interior with light. Traditional architectural elements are seen inside, including arches and columns, moldings and finials, and oak benches to create a familiar feeling. To break up this massive scale on the exterior, street level retail spaces were built to address the busy boulevard and make it more pedestrian-friendly. The exterior is a playful, colorful, visually busy cacophony of images mimicking traditional columns and capitals, cornices and moldings, in the Historic Eclectic Post-modern style, which reinterprets traditional architectural elements.

30) Westside Pavilion, 1985, The Jerde Partnership, 10800 West Pico Blvd.

Continue on Pico Blvd., left on Overland Avenue, right on Olympic Blvd.:

You are now approaching Century City, which was built on the 176-acre back lot of the 20th Century Fox Film Studios, which they sold off in the 1950s. Thriving 20th Century Fox studios still remain in the area. Most of the buildings went up in the 1960s through the 1990s. Century City is comprised mainly of office buildings, although there are both high-rise residences here and single-family homes. Some of the movie *Conquest of the Planet of the Apes* was filmed here and it was here that the fictitious Blue Moon Detective Agency of the "Moonlighting" TV series had their offices.

31) Once you turn onto Olympic Blvd., the skyscrapers of Century City are right in front of you. The Fox Plaza is the very tall tower you can see directly ahead, which was completed in 1987. With thirty-four stories, various angular forms create a multifaceted structure that is unified by a kind of skin composed of granite and glass with the color changing as it reflects the light of the sun. This building's Hollywood claim to fame is that it was the focal point of the *Die Hard* motion picture in 1989. Along with the Fox Plaza, Johnson Fain also designed the Sun America Center in 1990 at 1999 Avenue of the Stars and the MGM Tower on Constellation Boulevard, both high-rises here in Century City.

Born in northern California, Scott Johnson worked with the late architect Philip Johnson, to whom he is not related, in New York, but moved to Los Angeles in the early 1980s and worked with William Pereira, who designed many buildings in Los Angeles, one to be seen further along. He renamed Pereira's firm after William died to Johnson Fain.

31) Fox Plaza, 1987, Scott Johnson – Johnson Fain, 2121 Avenue of the Stars

Continue on Olympic Blvd.:

32) The two twin triangular shaped skyscrapers to the left of Fox Plaza were designed by the same architect who designed the twin towers of the World Trade Center in New York (1972 and 1973). There are obvious similarities of form and in the twin structures concept of this office building. From this vantage point, they look like towering, imposing structures that completely dwarf humans, which makes them even bolder. Surfaced in aluminum, the sheen of the towers makes them gleam in the sun as it is sets to the west behind you.

32) Century Plaza Towers, 1975, Minoru Yamasaki, 2029 & 2049 Century Park East

Right on Roxbury Drive:

33) Look to your left to the very top of this apartment building and you'll see a collection of variously colored shapes. Gehry designed this penthouse for artist Miriam Wosk. Inside, there are approximately 5,000 square feet of living space, 360 degree views, a private elevator, a sunken tub, steam shower, and fireplace in the master bedroom and two additional bedrooms. Originally, this was an ordinary four-story apartment building to which the top story was demolished to create this penthouse.

The budget for this residence was a little more than Gehry was accustomed to, so you do see the inclusion of some luxurious materials such as black granite. Other materials used here are wood, stucco, ceramic tile, and corrugated aluminum. The turquoise ceramic tile on the exterior shines in the sun in the living room and the circular kitchen behind is capped with a Moorish dome. The in-

congruous materials and forms create a visually exciting rooftop, wildly different from anything else in the neighborhood. The diverse shapes—domes, steps, curves, boxes—all work together to function as a home, which is a series of different, yet interlocking spaces lined up in a row with the living room on the west end with glass walls to take advantage of the views and the bedrooms at the back. The artist Miriam Wosk designed some of the interiors, with the encouragement of Gehry. You'll be able to see the back of it from Bedford Drive, looking behind 443 Bedford Drive.

33) Wosk House, 1984, Gehry Partners, 440 South Roxbury Drive

Continue around on Roxbury Drive, left on Bedford Drive, right on OlympicBlvd., left on LaCienega Blvd.:

34) Next, at the northwest corner of Olympic Blvd. and LaCienega Blvd. is the former Beverly Hills Waterworks. The Spanish Romanesque Revival style building was originally built in 1928 with a utilitarian function. It was water treatment plant no. 1. Designed by engineer Arthur Taylor to resemble a Mexican hacienda, the tower is a replica of the Giralda Tower in Seville, Spain. It is especially significant because it allowed Beverly Hills to be independent from the city of Los Angeles, as it has remained since 1914. It brought the water up from wells, but in 1976, the city of Beverly Hills began to purchase water from the L.A. Metropolitan Water District and the building was abandoned. It reopened in 1991 after an extensive restoration as the Margaret Herrick Library, part of the Academy of Motion Picture Arts & Sciences and is open to the public for research.

34) Beverly Hills Waterworks, (now Academy of Motion Picture Arts & Sciences Bldg. Margaret Herrick Library), 1928, Arthur Taylor, Restored 1991, Kaplin, McLaughlin & Diaz Architects, 333 South LaCienega Blvd.

Continue on LaCienega Blvd.:

35) At the southeast corner of LaCienega Blvd. and Wilshire Blvd. is the elliptically shaped brown glass office building originally built for Great Western Savings Bank. Sheathed in a glass curtain wall with a tiled plaza, the pure geometric form, extensive use of glass, and lack of ornamentation make it one of the classic iconic buildings of the International Style in Los Angeles. Placed on a diagonal to the street corner, the building addresses the intersection by its placement in the middle of the corner. Along with this structure, Pereira and Associates also designed the original Los Angeles County Museum of Art in 1964 and many other buildings around the city, including CBS Television City (Pereira and Luckman) at Fairfax Avenue and Beverly Blvd. and the Transamerica Pyramid in San Francisco.

This part of LaCienega Blvd. north of Wilshire Blvd. is called "Restaurant Row" due to the wide variety of restaurants on either side.

35) Great Western Savings Center Building, (now Flynt Publications), 1972, William Pereira & Associates, 8484 Wilshire Blvd. (above & right)

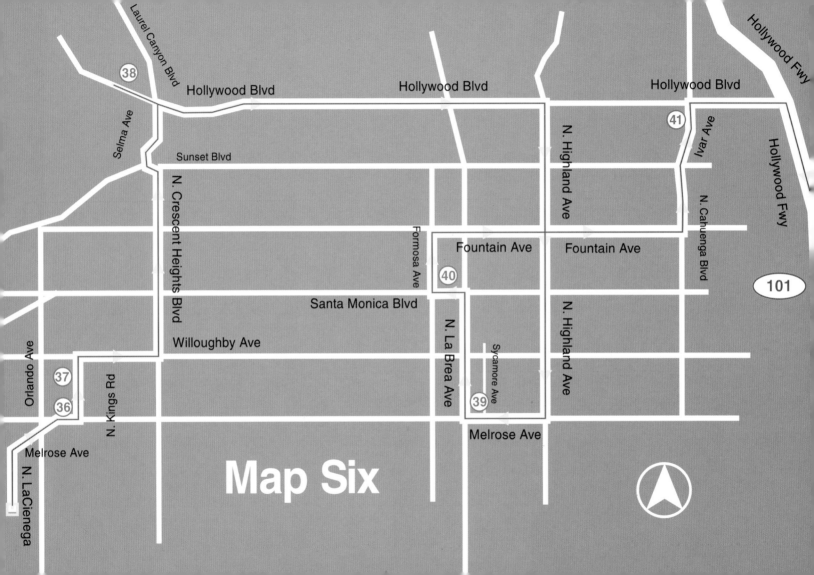

Laurel Canyon Blvd

38

Hollywood Blvd

Hollywood Blvd

Hollywood Blvd

Hollywood Fwy

Selma Ave

41

Ivar Ave

Hollywood Fwy

Sunset Blvd

N. Crescent Heights Blvd

N. Highland Ave

N. Cahuenga Blvd

101

Formosa Ave

Fountain Ave

Fountain Ave

40

Santa Monica Blvd

N. Highland Ave

Willoughby Ave

Orlando Ave

N. La Brea Ave

Sycamore Ave

37

N. Kings Rd

39

Melrose Ave

Melrose Ave

36

Map Six

Melrose Ave

N. LaCienega

![→] **Continue on LaCienega Blvd., right on Melrose Avenue:**

36) Past Orlando Avenue on your left is the Gemini G.E.L. (Graphic Editions Limited) print making studio and art gallery and a very good example of the early work of Gehry. Since the 1960s, a lithography studio was originally located here. The existing building is where the main entrance is covered in thick grey stucco. The two-story structure with printmaking studio space below and exhibition space above was added later. The exposed plywood studs are meant for you to see the "bones" of the structure, so windows were created to expose them. On the interior, the staircase is tilted slightly by a few degrees and in doing so heightens your awareness as you ascend. The idea that a building is more interesting before it's finished, when it is in the process of construction, one of Gehry's beliefs is in evidence here. One of the oldest galleries in Los Angeles, artists including Robert Rauschenberg, Roy Lichtenstein, Richard Serra, and many others have all come here to create multiples and display them here. This gallery is open to the public.

36) Gemini G.E.L., 1979, Gehry Partners, 8365 West Melrose Avenue

Left on Kings Road:

37) On your left behind the thick bamboo is the home of architect Rudolf M. Schindler. Made of tilt-up concrete, with varying levels and a flat roof, it has a communal kitchen and living room, and sleeping baskets, or porches, up above. Schindler also designed the outside spaces, using them as outdoor rooms. In this house, the architect redefines what a house is both in his use of space and materials and socially because this house was designed for two families to share. Notice the windows, which are mere vertical slits of glass and a result of the forms of the concrete wall. This is an abstraction and redefinition of what a window is. Here Schindler redefined what a house is, making it a truly Modern structure. The use of concrete throughout serves to keep the house cool in the warm southern California climate and the exterior spaces have been recessed to define outdoor rooms linking the inside to the outside.

Born and educated in Austria, Schindler came to Los Angeles as an employee of Frank Lloyd Wright's to supervise construction on the Hollyhock House (seen on the HOLLYWOOD tour). When that was finished he formed his own practice and this was the first house he built. This house is listed on the National Register of Historic Places and is now operated by MAK, an Austrian cultural organization, and is open to the public.

37) Schindler House, 1922, R.M. Schindler, 833 North Kings Road

Right on Willoughby Avenue, left on Crescent Heights Blvd., left on Sunset Blvd., right on Selma Avenue, left on Crescent Heights Blvd., right on Hollywood Blvd.:

38) Here on your left is one of the "textile block" houses designed by Frank Lloyd Wright in the early 1920s. It was originally built for homeopathic physician John Storer. The textile block system of construction was created by Frank Lloyd Wright and consisted of pouring concrete into patterned molds creating blocks and "stringing "them all together with steel reinforcing rod. Wright built four of these houses in southern California. (Two are seen on the HOLLYWOOD tour and the other on the PASADENA tour.) The textile block design is carried out on the interior of the house as well. The house is nearly 3,000 square feet inside and has three bedrooms and three bathrooms. Since 1984, the house was owned by movie producer Joel Silver and it was badly damaged in the 1994 6.6 Northridge Earthquake. Fortunately, it was fully restored with the help of grandson and architect Eric Lloyd Wright in 1995 and is maintained in good condition by another owner.

38) Storer House, 1923, Frank Lloyd Wright, 8161 Hollywood Blvd.

Continue on Hollywood Blvd. down the hill, cross Laurel Canyon Blvd., continue on Hollywood Blvd., past LaBrea Avenue, right on Highland Avenue, right on Melrose Avenue, right on Sycamore Avenue:

39) At the northwest corner of Sycamore Avenue and Melrose Avenue is a very early example of Gehry's work. Designed as a residence and studio for graphic designer Louis Danziger, the urban site was addressed by creating a blank privacy wall facing the street. Skylights and clerestory windows are used to get light into the home and studio and an interior courtyard provides a green oasis. The first application of exposed wood framing and ductwork was here, after which is seen repeatedly in Gehry's work. The influence of Modernism is seen here in the pure geometry of the form. The structure is composed of a series of cube forms, which when viewed straight on, are seen as a sculptural composition. Because Melrose Avenue is a busy street in a dense commercial area, the front is completely closed to the street; the windows and another entrance are around the back where it is more private. Thick walls also help to block out the street noise. The use of the thick stucco was originally intended to decrease the need for frequent painting; however, now it provides an irresistible surface for graffiti.

39) Danziger Studio, 1965, Gehry Partners, 7001 Melrose Avenue

Back out to Melrose Avenue heading west, right on La Brea Avenue, left on Santa Monica Blvd.:

40) Coming up quickly on your right, just past Detroit Street, is another very early example of Gehry's work. Another remodeling and expansion of an existing structure; a chrome plating factory in fact. It is one of Gehry's simplest and most industrial structures of all. Designed to house the factory and offices for this business, it is a series of box-like forms with an interesting logo on the front door. The expansion involved adding the second story, the construction of which was carried out without closing the factory operations.

40) Faith Plating Company, c. 1964, Gehry Partners, 7141 Santa Monica Blvd.

Right on Formosa Avenue, right on Fountain Avenue, left on Cahuenga Blvd., where road forks at Homewood Avenue, bear right onto Ivar Avenue, cross Sunset Blvd., just past Selma Avenue:

41) On your left is the Hollywood branch of the public library. Looking straight at the entrance, the placement of the box forms create a formal symmetry, not typical of Gehry's work. The original building on this location had been burned in a fire. The current massive central tower is flanked by two smaller ones, all at right angles and facing the street directly. Two smaller boxes each top the flanking towers with north-facing skylights. The cantilevered skylights here are the only indication of unease, more commonly seen in other structures. Built about twenty years after the Danziger Studio and Faith Plating Company, the library displays the new use of household materials in the blue ceramic bathroom tiles used on the exterior. A very light space has been created inside by use of the skylights. The interior features a circular stairwell leading up to the second floor to the large reading and reference area. This library services many people and was beginning to show signs of wear, so in 2006 a renovation was completed.

41) Frances Howard Goldwyn Regional Branch Library, c. 1986, Gehry Partners, 1623 Ivar Avenue

Right on Hollywood Blvd., pass Bronson Avenue and get on the Hollywood Freeway south to return to the Downtown L.A. starting point, exiting at Temple Avenue

Many new structures designed by Gehry Partners are currently being developed all over the world. In Los Angeles in 2007, a new high-rise complex directly across from Walt Disney Concert Hall on Grand Avenue was proposed. A mixed-use project, it will include two residential glass towers. One tower will be forty-seven stories and the other will be twenty-five stories high. A hotel, restaurants, and retail shops are also included in this proposal. The early design presentations show a contrast to the curvilinear shape and steel material of the concert hall. Instead, very tall rectilinear towers composed of glass will be shimmering across the street. Gehry will also be building his own house in Venice and has thus far received acceptance from the neighbors, who have seen the design drawings. Gehry has also designed furniture, watches, and a line of jewelry for Tiffany's.

From Gehry's early work in the 1960s to Walt Disney Concert Hall in the twenty-first century, a progression can be seen in each successive structure. A willingness to take risks and go beyond the accepted ways of thinking is what sets these buildings apart from any others. With a vocabulary of forms and materials, concepts and solutions are carried out and convey significance and meaning in late twentieth century and early twenty-first century urban life.

Some Additional Sites in the Southern California Area

Designed by Frank O. Gehry

- World Savings and Loan, 1980, 10064 Riverside Drive, North Hollywood
- Cabrillo Marine Museum, c. 1979, 3720 Stephen White Drive, San Pedro
- Team Disneyland Administration Building, 1987-1995, 800 West Ball Road, Anaheim
- Sirmai-Peterson House, 1988, 790 Calle Arroyo, Thousand Oaks
- Geffen Contemporary Museum-MOCA (originally the Temporary Contemporary), c. 1983, 152 North Central Avenue, Little Tokyo, Downtown Los Angeles
- California Aerospace Museum, c. 1984, Exposition Park, outskirts of Downtown Los Angeles

Selected Bibliography

The Architecture of Frank Gehry. Published on the occasion of an exhibition of the architect's major works, 1964 through 1986, organized by Walker Art Center, Minneapolis, Rizzoli, New York. Foreword by Henry N. Cobb, Essays by Rosemarie Haag Bleiter, Coosje van Bruggen, Mildred Friedman, Joseph Giovannini, Thomas S. Hines, Pilar Viladas; commentaries by Frank Gehry, 1986.

Chollet, Laurence B. *The Essential Frank O. Gehry.* New York, New York: The Wonderland Press, Harry N. Abrams, Inc., 2001.

Dal Co, Franceso and Kurt W. Forster. *Frank O. Gehry The Complete Works.* New York, New York: The Monacelli Press Inc., 1998.

Gebhard, David, and Robert Winter. *Los Angeles An Architectural Guide.* Layton, Utah: Gibbs Smith Publisher, 1994.

Pitt, Leonard and Dale Pitt. *Los Angeles A to Z An Encyclopedia of the City and County.* Berkeley, California: University of California Press, 1997.

Ragheb, J. Fiona, ed. *Frank Gehry, Architect.* Guggenheim Museum Publications, New York, New York: Harry N. Abrams Publishers, 2001.

Rubino, Luciano. *Frank O. Gehry Special.* Roma: Edizione Kappa, 1984.

Index of Architects

aARts William Dale Brantley Architects Inc., **36**
Becket, Welton and Associates, 27
Chu + Gooding, 10
DalyGenik (Kevin Daly & Chris Genik), 28
DMJM Design, 26
Ehrlich, Steven Architects, 44, 45
Ellwood, Craig, 31
Frederick Fisher and Partners, 37
Gehry Partners (Gehry, Frank), 6, 7, 9, 10, 11, **12**, 15, 17, 18, 19, 20, 21, 22, 23, 29, 32, 35, 37, **38, 46, 47, 52,** 57, 60, 61, 62
Graves, Michael, 43
Holland, William, 43
Howard, Ernest P. & Associates, 43
Isozaki, Arata with Gruen Associates, 12
Jerde Partnership, 49
Johnson Fain (Johnson, Scott), 50
Kaplin, McLaughlin & Diaz Architects, 53
Mack, Mark, Tim Sakamoto, Jeff Allsbrook, **40**
Marsh, Norman, 32
Mayne, Thom-Morphosis, 13, 14
Mulder/Katkov, 41
Murphy, Brian (BAM), 39
Parkinson, Donald and J.M. Estep, 25
Parr, George, 30
Pereira, William & Associates, 50, 54, 55
Reed, John G., Don E. Empakeris/REA Architects, 21
Russell, C.H., 32
Schindler, Rudolf M., 58
Taylor, Arthur, 53
Tyler, James, 31
Van Tilburg, Branvard & Soderbergh, 33, 34
Wright, Eric Lloyd, 59
Wright, Frank Lloyd, 58, 59
Yamasaki, Minoru, 51